Boxing Training

The Basic Boxing Fundamentals for Beginners

By Martin Gonzalez

© **Copyright 2023 - All rights reserved.**

The content contained within this book may not be reproduced, duplicated, or transmitted without direct written permission from the author or the publisher.

Under no circumstances will any blame or legal responsibility be held against the publisher, or author, for any damages, reparation, or monetary loss due to the information contained within this book, either directly or indirectly.

Legal Notice:

This book is copyright protected. It is only for personal use. You cannot amend, distribute, sell, use, quote, or paraphrase any part, or the content within this book, without the consent of the author or publisher.

Disclaimer Notice:

Please note the information contained within this document is for educational and entertainment purposes only. All effort has been executed to present accurate, up-to-date, reliable, and complete information. No warranties of any kind are declared or implied. Readers acknowledge that the author is not engaged in rendering legal, financial, medical, or professional advice. The content within this book has been derived from various sources. Please consult a licensed professional before attempting any techniques outlined in this book.

By reading this document, the reader agrees that under no circumstances is the author responsible for any losses, direct or indirect, that are incurred as a result of the use of the information contained within this document, including, but not limited to, errors, omissions, or inaccuracies.

DEDICATION

In life, there is always someone who lights your path, leads you toward your goals, and becomes your ideal.

In my journey of learning boxing as a sport,

I met my respected coach

Mr. Gene Vivero,

(1949-2021)

who ignited the fire and spirit within me to live life with pride and valor

and inspired me to continue the legacy of creating more efficient and capable boxers

by taking up boxing training.

I heartily dedicate this boxing book to my coach, guide, and mentor who made my life purposeful with his teachings and training.

Thank you!

Table of Contents

INTRODUCTION 1

CHAPTER ONE: BOXING AS A SPORTS 5
    WHAT IS BOXING? 6
    WHY SHOULD ONE OPT FOR BOXING AS A SPORT? 7
        Instills Defensive Art 8
        Boosts Our Self-Confidence 8
        Raises Kinesthetic Intelligence 9
    HOW DOES BOXING SERVE AS A BETTER SPORT? 9
    WHAT IS THE BEST AGE TO LEARN BOXING? 10

CHAPTER TWO: A BEGINNER'S BOXING TRAINING REGIME 11
    LIGHT STRETCHING 12
    RUNNING 13
    SKIPPING ROPE 13
    SHADOWBOXING 14
    HEAVY BAG WORKOUT 14
    DOUBLE-END BAG BOXING 15
    SPEED BAG BOXING 15
    PUSH-UPS 16
    SQUATS 16
    SIT-UPS 17

CHAPTER THREE: THE ESSENTIAL BOXING GEARS 19
    BOXING GLOVES 20
    HAND WRAPS 21
    BOXING HEAVY BAG 21
    BOXING HEAD GUARD 22
    BOXING MOUTH GUARD 22
    GROIN PROTECTOR AND CHEST GUARD 22
    BOXING SHOES 23
    BOXING SHORTS 23

CHAPTER FOUR: THE BASIC BOXING RULES 25

CHAPTER FIVE: IMPORTANT BOXING MOVES 29
    PUNCHING MOVES 30

- *The Jab*..30
- *The Cross* 31
- *The Hook*...31
- *The Uppercuts* 32

DEFENSIVE MOVES 33
- *Bobbing and Weaving* 33
- *Slipping* 34
- *Parrying* 35
- *Rolling*..35
- *Ducking Down*...36
- *Blocking* 37
- *Clinching* 37
- *Countering* 38

CHAPTER SIX: PERKS OF PRACTICING BOXING WORKOUTS 39

IMPROVES CARDIOVASCULAR HEALTH 40
BUILDS MUSCLES AND PHYSICAL STRENGTH 40
DEVELOPS ENDURANCE 41
ENHANCES MENTAL TOUGHNESS 41
HELPS MAINTAIN OVERALL FITNESS..42

CHAPTER SEVEN: TIPS TO LEARN BOXING FOR NEWBIES 43

FIGHT YOUR FEAR 44
FIND YOUR MOTIVATION...45
FOLLOW A GOOD COACH OR MENTOR 45
EAT A HEALTHY DIET...46

CHAPTER EIGHT: TALES OF FAMOUS BOXERS 49

MUHAMMAD ALI..50
MIKE TYSON 51
ROCKY MARCIANO 52
SONNY LISTON..52

BOXING MEMORIES... 55

CONCLUSION... 63

REFERENCES 65

IMAGE REFERENCES 67

Introduction

Just set yourself a goal and try and stick to it. Because you'll always end up better than where you started. —Anthony Joshua

In this ravishing world, the Divine has created a variety of living souls who are diverse from one another in almost all aspects. Some are happy-go-lucky, while some are sadistic; some are lively, while some are boring. Likewise, some are highly active while others prefer a sedentary lifestyle. So, depending on a person's personal choices, behaviors, and attitudes, we can distinguish everyone easily, which defines their identity and personality as an individual. When we think about people who prefer to be active, we also include a few of those who are health-conscious and fitness freaks. There are many different ways to maintain one's health and fitness like exercises, meditation, yoga, etc. But, one of the easiest and most fun-filled methods to stay active is by getting involved in some kind of physical sport. Among the list of various interesting sports, boxing has emerged as one of the most feasible and uncomplicated physical games that provides the benefits of exercising and workouts without putting in many resources.

For ages, people have been practicing boxing for different reasons, which has made boxing a very common sport. The ease of training and limited requirement of gear has made boxing people's favorite. When we talk about learning boxing, there is no particular age for it. One can learn boxing in their childhood as a hobby, or excel as a professional boxer in their later life, too. As with every other sport, even boxing demands proper training, which equips the newbies with the basic skills, strength, and stamina to fight bravely in the ring. Moreover, there are a set of specially designed protective gears, which a boxer needs to wear while getting trained as well as boxing matches. Using these essential gears reduces the chance of serious injuries that may even turn fatal in some cases.

Boxing is a game of passion, meant for those who love the sport and not their life. In this brutal sport, one has to be mentally and physically strong to receive the punches from the opponent, and there is always a risk of getting injured. In order to maintain discipline in the ring and prevent any sort of cheating, the game has a list of rules and regulations that are managed by the referee, who keeps a check on the different moves of the boxers. Talking of the moves, boxing has a few very unique techniques to punch the opponent, creating a huge blow. Apart from this, there are various defensive moves that a boxer employs to guard oneself against the fierce hit of the opponent boxer in the ring.

Despite the struggles and challenges that a boxer faces in the journey of becoming a boxing legend, there are a whole lot of advantages that boxing can yield in one's life. With the help and assistance of compatible trainers, learning to box becomes a cakewalk. In the haze of the hard-core punches delivered by the fighters, most of us often assume boxing to be a game of physical strength alone. But, in the course of understanding boxing in-depth, one can never overlook the mental toughness, endurance, and tolerance that it instills within us, thereby psychologically preparing us to bear the opponent's punches without breaking down. However, to beat the odds, there have to be some magical tips that can help the boxers become their best versions.

At times, the hardships on the path of learning boxing become so significant that one is compelled to change the direction of their life by giving up on their dreams and ambitions. But while looking at the lives of various great boxers like Muhammad Ali, Mike Tyson, Sonny Liston, etc., one can get loads of inspiration and positivity, which can again light the spark within them to own their dreams and fight against all the negativities that come on their way to become a strong and passionate boxer. So, let's move one step ahead in the journey to encompass our lives, with the power and goodness of boxing, and unveil the series of interesting questions that might be hovering in your minds at the moment:

- Is boxing made for me?

- Do I have the strength and toughness to become a boxer?

- Will boxing improve my lifestyle?

- What do I need to know to get started with boxing?
- What can I learn from the lives of the great boxers?

Chapter One:

Boxing as a Sports

Boxing is a science. You don't just walk into a gym and start punching. Fighters are born with differences in physical ability, but you also see a big difference in their skills. That's the trainer's influence at work. —Eddie Futch

It might be difficult to believe, but boxing is not a new sport for us, instead, it has been practiced since the time of our ancestors. Studies reveal that the history of boxing dates back to 3000 B.C. in Egypt, where the depictions created on the walls of tombs and the stone carvings hold evidence to prove the fact (Stone, 2020). In ancient times, people of Greece would wrap their fists in leather strips and fight with each other brutally. Boxing, which was earlier called the fisticuffs, was a popular sport in ancient Rome, too. You would have heard about gladiators, the Roman fighters who employed the same way of fighting by using leather strips wound around their fists along with metal blades plated on them. This made the fight savage and life-taking, which led to the abolition of such fist fights. Later, boxing resurfaced in Britain in the 16th century as a means of sorting conflicts, where rich patrons would hire fighters and put huge bets on their win. This is how the concept of prizefighting was introduced, thus, reintroducing the tradition and trend of boxing in history.

The first boxing school was opened up by Jack Broughton, an English boxer, who also introduced the first basic set of boxing rules and invented mufflers to protect one's hand from injuries while boxing. He was the one who motivated people to become fighters themselves, rather than promoting sponsored fighting. At that time, during the early 19th century, boxing was a very unpopular sport in America. Theodore Roosevelt, former United States President, advocated the need for training his officers in boxing, as he believed that boxing is the best way to vent out the animal spirit within oneself (Dilbert, 2017). Apart from this, he himself practiced boxing daily, as a means to keep himself fit, active, strong, and in good shape. This became the turning point in the history of boxing, as it made the sport spread worldwide at a faster pace, making it one of the most liked physical sports by the people.

What Is Boxing?

Boxing is a type of combat sport that involves two opponents each strategically punching the other one, while at the same time, it is a struggle to defend themselves from the attack of retrieving punches by the opponent boxer. Boxing is also called pugilism, which means "fist-fight", thus it is a fight that incorporates fighting with fists. This fist-fight is a form of sport that usually takes place inside an enclosed area, called the ring. During each boxing round, a referee is assigned to stay inside the rings and keep a watch on the players to check that the rules are followed properly and that no boxer is playing foul in the sport. The winner of the boxing match held between the two fierce opponents is decided after the completion of a series of timed rounds. The judges outside the ring are appointed to decide the winner, based on the comparison of the total points earned by the two boxers. Many times, the champion is decided when one of the participants is knocked out of the game by the other boxer.

Modern boxing is basically classified into two basic types—amateur boxing and professional boxing. Amateur boxing is beginner-level boxing, which advocates wearing protective headgear while the match is on. In this type of boxing, the scores are granted based on the simple calculation of points earned by each of the boxers, rather than the intensity of physical damage caused by the opponent boxer. These matches are generally of shorter duration as compared to professional boxing matches, comprising three rounds of three minutes each, with a rest of one minute in between each round. On the contrary, professional boxing, which is aimed at prizefighting, is not as easy as amateur boxing, since it stretches longer and has 10 to 12 rounds in each match. Moreover, in this type of boxing, the fighters are not allowed to wear any protective headgear, which causes more damage to the participating fighters. Furthermore, in professional boxing, the winner is not decided based on the mere calculation of points, instead, the boxer who knocks out the opponent in the ring becomes the champion.

Why Should One Opt for Boxing as a Sport?

Even the thought of learning boxing or becoming a pro fighter in this hard-hitting sport can give you goosebumps, and make you feel anxious and even spooked out. Watching a fistfight between two pro boxers often includes lots of throwing and taking of punches upon each other, which may even cause deadly physical and brain injuries, at times. However, if one is willing to opt for boxing as a fitness sport, leisure activity, or due to an urge of developing unmatched strength and health goals, then it can turn out to be an amazing option for you. Thus, in order to learn the best skills from this sport, it is a must to select the correct way of training oneself and grasping the basic details that are crucial to gain excellence as a boxer. Apart from the tremendous benefits boxing can render, it is a sport that can help you redefine your personality both physically and mentally. So, let's have a look at the various factors that compel one to choose boxing as a passionate sport in their life.

Instills Defensive Art

Life is always unpredictable, as any challenge or difficulty never approaches us with a forewarning. So, we should always be mentally prepared to face such situations, which can create turmoil in our life. Thus, in order to build mental toughness and gain control over one's emotions, one can practice the sport of boxing, which can inculcate the ability and strength to stand strong and defend oneself. Boxing, which is one of the oldest forms of martial art, is the best way to adapt the qualities of controlling one's movements, striking the opponent at the right time, and defending oneself from any sudden attacks. However, this wonderful technique of self-preparing oneself cannot be instilled in a night, instead, it requires genuine effort, consistency, and dedication. Thus, understanding the act of punching the opponent at the right time and with perfect speed, is the key boxing skill that can instill defensive behavior in us thereby, changing our perception toward our life too.

Boosts Our Self-Confidence

A common problem that almost all of us face in our life is confronting a big crowd or feeling very confident in front of many people, which proves to be a challenging situation. However, learning a sport like boxing can expose us to large masses cheering and yelling at us. This in turn can automatically enhance our self-confidence, thereby making us more capable to form better perceptions and ideas about ourselves. Indulging in this unique martial art form can assist in forming our strong identity, which can ignite the hidden positivity within us. Although this sport demands a lot of physical stability and power to fight against the opponent boxer, it also affects our mental strength and thought process, too. Thus, boxing prepares us best, for the unseen circumstances that may create fear, anxiety, and awkwardness within us; to engage with unknown people and handle unanticipated issues of life, effortlessly.

Raises Kinesthetic Intelligence

Kinesthetic intelligence may seem to be an alien term for many of us, but for those who are obsessed with boxing, it is something that intelligently defines the science of mind-body union. As boxing demands a person to efficiently coordinate their mind and body movements, it improves the response time of the senses, thereby helping one to take the right decision at the right moment. Boxing is a versatile sport that works miraculously to enhance one's spatial awareness, physical presence, and eye-hand coordination. Thus, learning and practicing boxing can help us become smart, quick-witted, and agile, thereby preparing our mind and body to work more skillfully and effectively, even during tough times.

How Does Boxing Serve as a Better Sport?

Boxing is a universal martial art that not only supports one to build their career in the field of sports, but also helps in learning interesting moves, which can be enjoyed as a hobby, or even practiced as a fun-filled fitness regime. Out of the different ways, one way to practice boxing is to do it on a punching bag as a boxing workout, to keep oneself physically fit. So, let's discover the various aspects of boxing that make it one of the best options to help you stay fit.

1. Boxing is a type of exercise that helps in boosting aerobic fitness, which is good to improve one's heart health. It is a form of high-intensity interval training that is known to reduce the risk of various heart diseases.

2. Boxing is an interesting way to indulge yourself in a fun sport that can automatically help you lose lots of weight efficiently. When you practice boxing as a routine, it helps in burning extra calories and works to reduce body fats, which is even more effective than a brisk walk.

3. This heavy-duty sport helps in improving the entire body's strength by working on the core muscles as well as the lower limbs of your body.

4. This martial art is more of a movement-intensive sport, which helps in improving the coordination of the hand and footwork. It enhances the ability of the body to develop reactive strategies against sudden changing conditions and also boosts muscle strength. These factors are the key to improving one's balance.

5. Sometimes, giving a full-intensity throw at the punching bag is a better way to relieve the stress from your mind, which may make you feel liberated, and improves your mood.

What Is the Best Age to Learn Boxing?

Boxing is a healthy sport that has no restriction of age limit. It is never too late to begin the journey of boxing if one is looking for an exciting opportunity to enlist a new hobby, practice it as an exercise regime, boost mental and physical strength, or simply work positively toward boosting their self-confidence and self-esteem. Although, if one is willing to choose boxing as a career option and become a pro at throwing the punches, then the ideal age is to begin as early as possible. The best age to start boxing is around seven to eight years of age. Young age is the most feasible time to practice a martial art like boxing as it helps in grasping the vital qualities necessary to become a successful boxer, like discipline, endurance toward good habits, physical strength, stamina, and muscle memory.

Chapter Two:

A Beginner's Boxing Training Regime

Training fighters is like trying to catch a fish. It's a technique, not strength. — Angelo Dundee

In a race to maintain one's fitness and pursue the dream to become a boxer, one fails to understand the importance of a consistent training regime, which is crucial for excelling in the sport of boxing. There are many people who practice boxing as a hobby and do not need strict training. However, those who wish to become a rising star in the ring do need regular and disciplined training, by expert coaches or trainers. As a beginner, one simply needs to understand that every training process must go slow and steady in order to achieve the desired outcome. So, let's uncover the simple and basic exercises and workouts that are a must for beginner boxing enthusiasts to gain name and fame as efficient boxers.

Light Stretching

Stretching is important before you begin any kind of exercise, even boxing. Stretching each time you begin boxing can help in reducing the chances of getting injuries or muscle pulling. Stretching is basically of two types: dynamic stretching and static stretching. Dynamic boxing stretching is simply moving your body consistently and actively, intending to warm up your muscles. These stretching exercises are performed before boxing, and not after that. While static boxing stretching is the common stretching that involves pulling a joint or muscle to its maximum stretch point for at least 10 to 20 seconds. The main aim of doing static stretching is to increase blood flow, which helps in soothing the muscles after boxing. Therefore, this stretching is often performed after boxing and not before that. There are three different ways to perform dynamic stretching that can be done before each boxing routine.

Arm stretching: One of the simplest methods to gear up for boxing is to begin with arm stretching, as it involves all the muscles of the upper thorax and arms. These muscles are the ones that assist a boxer in giving a hard blow or punch to the opponent, thereby breaking their bones and morale, as well.

Back stretching: Back stretching is the best way to prepare your back muscles and spine to bear the impact of punches delivered by the opponents and provide perfect bounce to strike the other boxers.

Hip circles: Hip circles help in warming up the hip muscles, which form an essential part of the twisting motions that helps throwing efficient boxing strikes.

Running

Running is a basic exercise that helps in building stamina by improving cardio-pulmonary and cardiovascular fitness. Running must be included as an integral part of your morning routine that helps in inculcating discipline and shedding extra kilos. Apart from building stamina, running each morning can also help in improving the explosiveness within a person that induces the required energy for throwing punches. Further, running regularly can also boost your mental endurance and determination to perform your best. As a beginner, you can start by running at least half a mile a day. During this time one can try running for a few meters and then opt for sprinting for a few meters which helps to improve your aerobic fitness, speed, and strength.

Skipping Rope

Skipping rope is the best way to promote cardio-vascular workouts, which makes it an integral part of boxing. Skipping helps in warm-ups and cool-downs before you begin your boxing training. The best part about skipping is that one can practice it at any place and at any time without the need to hit the gym. Skipping helps in improving footwork, quickness, and speed and boosts physical stamina and muscle strength. Further, skipping is an aerobic exercise that enhances mental stamina, conditions the mind, and builds mental toughness in boxers. Practicing skipping as a routine can also help in improving one's coordination as it simultaneously involves and promotes the function of legs, eyes, and arms to skip the swinging rope. As a beginner, one must try skipping for two minutes completing two rounds each, which can be increased gradually based on one's strength, stamina, and comfort.

Shadowboxing

Shadowboxing is one of the easiest and best exercises for a beginner, which must be done even before you try boxing on a heavy bag, sparring session, or pad work. Shadowboxing can be practiced without the need for any equipment and at any place. The main reason behind practicing shadowboxing is to introduce oneself to the basic movements of boxing punches. Practicing shadowboxing fights helps in improving mental strength as it supports mirroring a fight. Every boxer practices shadowboxing as it is a feasible and straightforward way of boosting one's speed, power, coordination, and muscle memory. If you ignore practicing this step, there are chances that you feel tense and panic out in the actual fights as it prepares your mind for the final battle.

The best way to begin shadowboxing is to perform two rounds each for two minutes, while it is important to establish and understand your goals before you start. To achieve the best result, start with throwing one punch drill at a time like jabs, hooks, uppercuts, or crosses. Later, when you develop confidence and coordination, you can try coordinating two or more punch drills at a time like jab-cross, jab-cross-lead hook, or double jab-cross.

Heavy Bag Workout

Learning boxing with the help of a heavy bag can help in gaining expertise in throwing punches. It also improves muscle strength, aids muscle toning, enhances coordination, liberates stress, and also burns out calories. Along with being an exciting and fun exercise, heavy bag workout supports developing rhythm and coordination. There is no strict rule when it comes to practicing heavy bag punching. However, beginners can practice two rounds for two minutes each. One can increase the rounds and duration based on their fitness level, ease, and comfort. Before each heavy bag work session you must do a quick warm-up that includes skipping, arm circles, hip circles, and lunges.

Further, using boxing gloves and hand wraps can help in protecting you from getting injury and strain. Some of the easy heavy bag workout drills are coordination of various punch drills like, "double jab-left hook-bob and weave", "jab-cross-left body shot-right body shot", and "straight punches-power body shots".

Double-End Bag Boxing

A double-end bag is a versatile piece of equipment that not only helps beginners but also professionals practice their boxing sport. A beginner can easily notice an improvement in their stamina, coordination between eyes and hands, and also between the upper and lower body. Including a double-end bag into the daily routine can help a beginner to hold command to throw punches in combination, like jab-cross. It also improves boxer's punching accuracy, timing, speed and rhythm, rapid reflexes, striking power, and footwork. Double-end bags are available in various sizes and shapes. However, choosing an eight to nine inches double-end bag with medium cords can help a beginner learn smoothly and comfortably. A beginner must start by practicing at least two rounds of double-end bag punches for two minutes each. Gradually, when you gain expertise, you can increase the number of rounds. As a beginner, you must begin with throwing light punches and easy combinations like jab-cross, jab-jab-cross, or jab-jab.

Speed Bag Boxing

Speed bag boxing is another method to build one's stamina and endurance. This equipment is quite different from other bags, as it is hung at a smaller distance from the ceiling, which supports quick rebounding. Practicing different boxing drills on a speed bag can help in improving steadiness, building accuracy, supporting speed control, and learning better pacing techniques. Apart from this, using speed bags also improves cardiovascular health, by increasing the heart rate, thereby lowering the risk of various cardiovascular diseases and also burning extra calories. As a beginner, one must opt for doing two rounds of speed bag punching, with different punching drills for at least two minutes each. Each round must be repeated at a gap of at least 30 seconds to one minute.

Push-Ups

Push-ups are compound exercises that involve the movement of multiple muscle groups of the body at the same time, which helps boxers to engage their pectoral muscles, triceps, shoulders, core muscles, and lower back. Thus, aids in maintaining their upper body and its core strength. However, experts recommend doing only one or two sets of 50 push-ups each day. As boxing requires the use of muscles in front of the arms and shoulders, doing many sets of push-ups at a time, can add more strenuous work on the front upper body, resulting in severe fatigue and injuries. Many variations in the push-ups like knuckle push-ups, alternating medicine ball push-ups, plyometric push-ups, clap push-ups, etc., can efficiently help in improving the punching skills and strength of the boxer.

Squats

Like in many other sports, squats are very helpful in boxing too. Including squats in one's regular exercise regime can help in toning and strengthening the muscles like gluteus, hamstrings, and quads. It also helps improve stability and core strength, which altogether supports the movements involved in throwing punches. As a beginner, one must not exceed 50 squats per day, as it may lead to muscle spasms and discomfort. There are many variants of squats that can work in improving the speed and intensity of a boxer's punch. For instance, jump squats help develop an explosive force that powers the punch, while squat jacks help in improving footwork by adding stability. Further, another type of squats that involves compound movements is dumbbell thrusters, which focus on the lower body along with the tricep and trapezoid muscles, thereby strengthening the entire body.

Sit-Ups

An important type of abdominal exercise that helps a boxer to throw powerful punches and strengthen their core, while also improving their balancing and stability, is sit-ups. It is an easy set of exercises that can help a boxer improve their body movements, get rid of back pains, and provide muscular endurance. More than focusing on the counts, it is necessary to do sit-ups at proper intervals. Beginners can start by doing three sets of sit-ups for two minutes each or three sets of 50 sit-ups once or twice a day. If one finds it difficult to do these sit-ups at a stretch, then one can plan its feasibility by doing one round of sit-ups in the morning and the second round in the evening.

Chapter Three:

The Essential Boxing Gears

Boxing isn't just about brute strength; it's about skill and outwitting your opponent.
—Lennox Lewis

Luckily, boxing is a sport that does not require much groundwork and expenses to get started with the learning process. Boxing is a physically arduous and tough sport that mandates the beginners to have the right set of equipment or gears, in order to ensure their safety and triumph in the ring. Various boxing gears are specially designed for this sport and are essential for boxers to perform their best, protect themselves from fatal injuries, and enhance their dexterities. While training as a newbie in boxing, one will undergo two types of training—with and without the partner; depending on which, the gears may vary a bit. Thus, selecting the perfect set of boxing gear that supports the boxer's comfort is a must. Moreover, these boxing gears can be customized to fit the boxer best, so that there is no scope for any mishappening in the ring. So, let's explore and discuss the different basic boxing gears that every boxer must aim to have in order to mark their unanimous win in the boxing ring.

Boxing Gloves

Boxing gloves are one of the most vital gears for any boxer, be it a beginner under training or a boxing legend. However, choosing the right pair of boxing gloves is a highly debated topic, as there are two types of boxing gloves available. One is the training or bag gloves and the other is the sparring or competition gloves, which are used depending on the level of boxing one aims to opt for. Boxing gloves also come in different sizes, weights, and styles, depending on the boxer's skill level, weight, and personal choice. There are a few necessary things one needs to consider while selecting a pair of boxing gloves for oneself:

- lightweight
- good material
- perfect fit
- supports flexibility

Considering the cost is an important factor, but while doing so, compromising the quality of gloves will land you purchasing a new pair just after a few practicing sessions. The main purpose of wearing boxing gloves is to protect one's hands from injuries and to provide cushioning, which eventually reduces the impact of punches on opponents.

Hand Wraps

Hand wraps are another essential piece of gear that every boxer needs to have. They are basically designed to protect the smaller bones of your hands, wrists, and knuckles to refrain from any sort of severe injuries during training or fights. Moreover, hand wraps also provide extra support and stability to the wrists while punching, thus making them less susceptible to sprains and strains. These hand wraps also increase the life of your gloves, as they absorb all the sweat and the blood that would otherwise spoil the gloves. There are many different types of hand wraps available for boxers, depending on their size and style of wrapping that a boxer prefers. Some hand wraps are made up of elastic material, which offers a tighter grip, extra comfort, and a perfect fit. Apart from this, there are special slip-on hand wraps designed for beginners that make it easier to use, thereby avoiding the issue of wrapping it around your hands. Thus, hand wraps are the key to ensuring maximum protection and support while boxing.

Boxing Heavy Bag

When it comes to a boxing heavy bag, it is not a must requirement for all the newbies under training. Those who prefer a gym for practicing their boxing skills need not spend a penny on arranging a heavy bag, as it is already available there. However, those who pursue boxing as a hobby or a passion may get a heavy bag for themselves to burn their extra calories by punching on the heavy bag at home. There are a large variety of options open for selecting a heavy bag, based on its weight, the material that is filled inside the bag, the material of the cover, etc. However, it is recommended to choose a punching bag made of vinyl, as it is more durable and can withstand heavy blows. Moreover, a heavier punching bag is usually preferred, as it will not bounce back when you hit a hard punch on it. Nowadays, the foam filling inside the heavy bags is replaced by water, which provides better firmness while practicing punching.

Boxing Head Guard

Boxing head guard is an important requirement for boxers, as it protects the boxer from the impact of heavy punches on the head and face area delivered by the opponents in the ring. Apparently, it is designed to guard the boxer's head, but unfortunately, it cannot prevent fatal brain injuries during the match. Thus, the quality of the head guard selected does matter, as it improves the level of protection provided. These protective headgears come in different sizes and styles, depending on the boxer's personal choice, head size, and the protection needed. Moreover, the boxer should know the correct way of wearing a head guard, so that it stays in place as the boxer receives the punches. The boxing head guard should fit on the head properly, providing comfort and allowing the boxer to hear and see clearly during the match.

Boxing Mouth Guard

In boxing, a mouth guard is as essential as a boxing glove, as it is specially made to safeguard the boxer's lips, teeth, and jaws from getting severely damaged while receiving different boxing punches like a jab or an uppercut in a match. A boil-and-bite mouth guard, made up of EVA, is designed to provide a better fit, as it can be easily molded according to the jawline of different boxers. Thus, a proper fit of the mouth guard should be ensured before jumping into the ring for a big fight, as it will prevent any severe mouth injuries and reduce the impact of the punches, too.

Groin Protector and Chest Guard

One of the most overlooked pieces of boxing gear in boxing is the groin protector and the chest guard, as they are uncomfortable to wear and restrict one's mobility. But, it is very important to wear a chest guard in the ring, especially for the new boxers, as it protects one from chest injuries that can break the ribs and even damage various internal organs, leading to death. Moreover, a groin protector that is designed for male boxers guards the sensitive lower portion of the boxer. Initially, it may be a bit difficult to fight with these complicated gears, but with consistent practice, one gets habitual to it.

Boxing Shoes

As we all know, boxing is not just the game of punching and defending oneself, instead, it demands a whole lot of footwork to create the perfect balance and stability. Thus, special boxing shoes are designed to help the boxer build maximum mobility and bounce in the ring. One thing that a beginner boxer must look out for in a boxing shoe, is that they should be weightless, flexible, and provide a skid resistance sole to ensure good movements and traction in the boxing ring. A good-fit boxing shoe ensures enhanced performance by the boxer and even reduces the risk of foot and ankle injuries while in the match.

Boxing Shorts

Boxing shorts are an optional thing that a boxer can easily arrange in order to feel comfortable and maintain flexibility while in the match. These special boxing shorts are made of lightweight and breathable fabric, which provides ample room for movement. The color and size of the boxing shorts completely depend on the choice of the boxer.

Chapter Four:

The Basic Boxing Rules

Boxing is a sport of self-control. You must understand fear so you can manipulate it. Fear is like fire. —Cus D'Amato

Boxing, which marked its existence as a gruesome sport in history, is now considered a rewarding yet intimidating game, which attracts the attention and interest of many boxing lovers. Moreover, the fascinating journey of learning boxing is further enhanced by the strenuous efforts of the trainers and mentors. Apart from this, the series of rules and regulations defined for boxing make it a fairly played game that wins millions of hearts with each punch. These rules and regulations surely help us learn the strategies of the game more deeply and thus become a reason for enjoying every bit of it to the fullest. So, let's dive deeper into the game of boxing, to understand and learn the different rules that make boxing a marvelous sport.

1. Boxing is of two different types—amateur boxing and professional boxing.

2. Amateur boxing continues for three rounds, while professional boxing involves at least nine to 12 rounds in a match.

3. In both types of boxing, each round has a break of one minute in between. The fighter can prepare themselves for the next round during this one-minute break by going to their respective corners allotted in the ring.

4. Each fighter is allotted a corner of the ring, from where they make the entry when the boxing match starts.

5. During the break, each fighter can rest at their respective corners in the ring where they can have water, talk to their coach, or adjust their boxing gloves.

6. Each boxing game is supervised by an appointed referee, who ensures that the boxers play the game fairly.

7. In order to have a fair boxing game, a panel of three judges is selected, who award points to each fighter based on their defense moves, punches thrown, and knockdowns.

8. In a match, when the result is decided on the basis of awarded points, it often ends up in a draw. However, in this scenario, if a fighter knocks out their opponent, they can have an easy win.

9. A knockout is a situation when a fighter is knocked down by the opponent in the ring and is the basic criterion for deciding the champion of the match. In such a case, the referee counts to ten, and if the knocked-down player doesn't stand up, he is declared the loser, thereby ending the game.

10. In boxing, groin-area strikes are strictly prohibited, as they can be extremely painful and may result in irreparable damage to the player.

11. In a boxing match, the boxer must be mindful of not holding the opponent fighter, while throwing punches over him.

12. The boxers are not allowed to exhibit violent moves and gestures like spitting, biting, shoving, and tripping toward their opponents.

13. This sport does not permit any unethical behavior to be shown by its players like striking the opponent with your arm, kicking them, or headbutting them.

14. Once the referee interferes in the match, by breaking the player's clinch, it is a must for each fighter to take one full step backward before they punch their opponent again.

15. In case, if a boxer gets knocked down, they must move to a neutral corner inside the ring until the referee gives a new instruction to them.

16. If any of the boxers fail to follow the boxing rules, their action is declared to be foul. Depending on the type of foul play, the player receives a warning from the referee, which results in a deduction of their earned points.

17. If a fighter commits severe foul play, it can lead to disqualification from the match itself. Furthermore, committing a foul play intentionally in order to hinder the smooth flow of the game may lead to their elimination from the championship.

18. If a boxer gets severely injured and is unable to return to the ring, they are considered to be knocked out of the match.

19. When a fighter sustains a fatal injury that occurs due to a foul move, the game is considered no contest. Sometimes, the fight's results are determined based on the awarded points and the rounds played by each fighter.

20. The only permitted move in boxing is to throw a punch with a clenched fist. Moreover, hitting below the belt near the kidneys, or the back of an opponent, is strictly forbidden and is considered foul play.

21. During a boxing match, the fighter is not allowed to hold the rope surrounding the ring, in order to take support.

22. In a boxing match, if a boxer is punched with a low blow, a minimum time span of five minutes is given to them in order to rest and recover from it.

23. Once a fighter is knocked down in a match, they are not allowed to hit their opponent.

24. In case a referee prompts a break signal, then it is a must for both fighters to oblige and refrain from punching each other.

Chapter Five:

Important Boxing Moves

To be a great champion you must first believe you are the best. If you're not, pretend you are. —Muhammad Ali

Boxing may not seem to be a very sophisticated game. However, looking at great professionals, fighting in the ring may leave one awestruck for a moment. The high level of physical strength, endurance, and mental toughness exhibited by these legends, justify their love and passion for boxing. For newbies who wish to gain expertise in boxing, it is a necessary step to closely watch the different moves and styles of fighting displayed by various famous boxers. This can help beginners to master the art of perfection in boxing and can assist in learning each of the moves effortlessly. So, let's take the boxing craze to the next level, by unveiling the tricks behind different boxing moves.

Punching Moves

Sometimes, it is mesmerizing, as well as at the same moment encouraging, to watch your favorite professional fighters showcasing the pinnacle of their boxing skills, while it can also make the beginners feel intimidated by the kind of moves and the punches that they throw. However, these boxing techniques and moves are not miracles or a kind gift from the Divine. Instead, it is the fruitful result of their hard work, consistent efforts, and determination that pays them off at the end of the match. So, let's explore and make ourselves familiar with the fundamental moves that form the four main types of boxing punches.

The Jab

Jab is the basic yet most effective and safest punching technique that can have a huge impact on an opponent. This punch is usually thrown with the lead hand from a guard position and delivers a high-speed, straight punch toss. This punching technique is considered a vital skill in a boxer's arsenal as it provides a good amount of personal spread, which leaves less room for an opponent to counterattack the throw. Most professional boxers use the jab as a range finder, but it can also be used in combination with other punching techniques.

The Cross

If you are looking to add precision and power while throwing a punch, you must opt for hitting a cross. The cross is a straightforward, strong, and effective punch that is thrown with the backhand or rear (strong) hand. This punching technique is more powerful than the jab, and also the second safest punching trick in a boxer's arsenal. It can be used as a ranged weapon. A high-intensity and strong cross has enough potential to keep an opponent away and restrict them to counterattack.

The Hook

The hook is a strong and high-powered semicircular punch that supports a boxer to punch the side of the opponent's body or head with extensive force and thrust. This punching technique gains strength from your torso and legs, while its range is limited from middle to inside. Learning this type of punching technique could be tricky for a beginner, as it makes use of the weak hand to throw punches. However, with consistent efforts and great practice, one can gain the expertise to throw this powerful punch and take the lead in a boxing fight.

The Uppercuts

Uppercut is a technique that helps a boxer to knock out their opponent. This punching technique uses the rear or the backhand to throw a vertical and rising punch at the opponent. As this punch uses an upward trajectory to attack the opponent, it makes it difficult to block and leaves no space for them to counterattack. Uppercuts are used when you have to attack the opponent at a closer distance. The movement of the leg and torso provides the power to punch an uppercut by driving the fist into the opponent.

Defensive Moves

Often we believe that offense is the only crucial part of learning boxing skills that include throwing a combination of punches, striking powerful punches to knock out the opponent, and hitting a hard counterpunch to your opponent to take the lead in the game. However, boxing is a sport that could let you taste defeat if one fails to instill the right defense technique. Defense is a vital component of boxing which helps in lowering the morale of your opponents inside the boxing ring and discourages them to strike an effective and powerful punch. Many eminent personalities in the field of boxing like Muhammad Ali, Pernell Whitaker, and Floyd Mayweather Jr. have developed unbeatable and exceptional defense skills which became the major reason for their magnificent victories. However, developing defensive skills can be challenging in the initial days, especially for beginners. So, let's dive deep and explore a plethora of astounding defensive boxing skills that can act as a game changer for you.

Bobbing and Weaving

Head movement lays the foundation for developing a skillful defense called bobbing and weaving. The main idea behind this defense trick is to distract the fighter to attack the target by constantly shifting the head position from one side to the other, up and down, at varied paces and patterns. This defense trick makes it harder, more erratic, and more hesitant for an opponent to throw powerful punches. Bobbing and weaving is the key to framing an effective defensive strategy, as it can disrupt the rhythm of the opponent to ruin their entire game. The best way to gain expertise in this defensive move is to practice it as much as you can with your trainer, alone, or during shadowboxing.

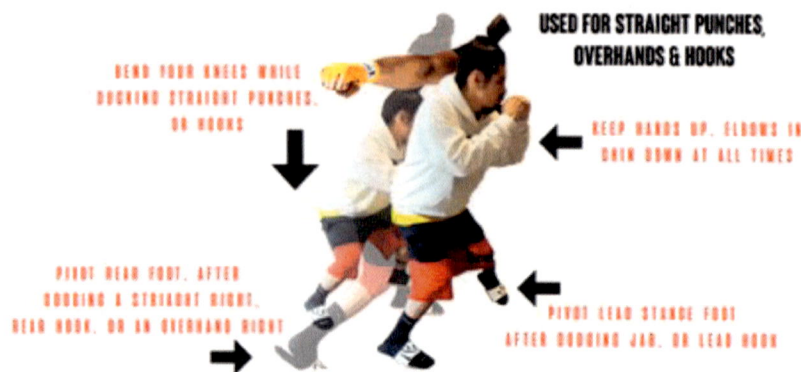

Slipping

As the name suggests, the main thought behind slipping punches is to develop sharp reflexes to anticipate the opponent's attack and take a smart move. With this reactionary defense tactic, you can slip your head either to the right or the left depending upon the opponent's punch, to cause them to miss their shot. At this moment in time, it is important to take the lead and counter strike your opponent with the right punch, as the opponent would not be prepared for it. Slipping is focused on doing the right head moves at the right time, therefore it needs immense training and practice either with a trainer or by doing shadowboxing.

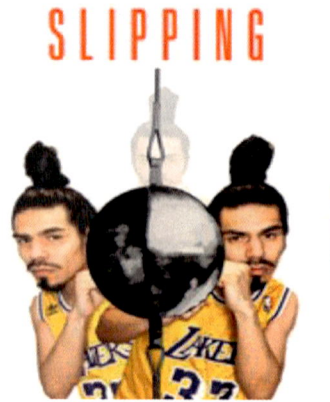

Parrying

Parrying can prove to be a crucial and most advantageous weapon in a boxer's arsenal, as it dramatically shifts the game in your favor. Parrying is the use of your hands to deflect and divert the punching shots of the opponent, which redirects the trajectory, focus, and motion of the punch and causes the opponent to miss it. This is the best time to set a devastating counter-attack as the opponent is left wide open, clueless, and vulnerable.

USED FOR PUSHING AWAY OPPONENTS PUNCHES FROM IT'S ORIGINAL DESTINATION

Rolling

Rolling is a modified type of parrying technique in which a boxer uses their body instead of their hands to deflect an opponent's punch. Rolling the shoulders is an effective way to avoid an offense from the opponent as well as to counter-attack them as your hands are free to throw a punch. It is a feasible technique to save your entire body as well as the head from effective, powerful, and multiple attacks. However, beginners can face issues when using a rolling defensive strategy, as failure to recognize the right direction of the attack can hint you to roll on the wrong side. Also, rolling is not very effective when a fast-speed punch is thrown like that of a jab, which is the most common style of punching the majority of the time.

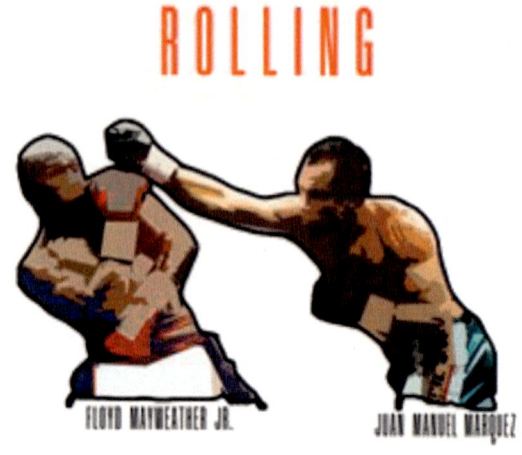

ADAPTING TO THE DIRECTION OF YOUR OPPONENTS PUNCHES TO LOWER IMPACT

Ducking Down

Ducking is one of the easiest and simple boxing defense techniques that can be learned with no hassle, but the successful trick lies in the fact that you execute this trick at the right time and correctly to reduce the impacts of shots and avoid injuries. Many reasons make ducking a demanding defense technique, since it helps you avoid the most intimidating and powerful punches of the opponent boxer. Further, ducking is a feasible defense technique as it helps you avoid punch without losing the balance, while in other defensive tricks like weaving and slipping there are chances that you lose your balance as much tilting and shifting is required. Ducking down is the best option for a beginner to inculcate within themselves as a prime defense mechanism because it serves various benefits over other techniques like maintaining balance, is easy to learn, eases a counter-defense punch, and it's a simple way to let your opponent's punch go null and void.

DUCKING DOWN

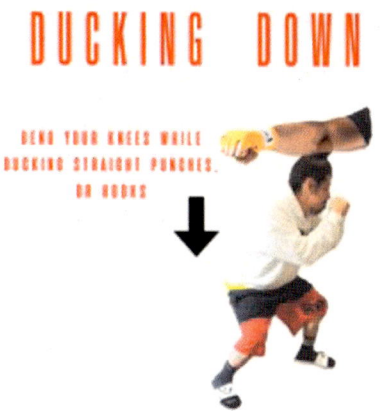

BEND YOUR KNEES WHILE DUCKING STRAIGHT PUNCHES OR HOOKS

Blocking

Blocking is a defensive technique in which you are in direct physical contact with your opponent, unlike the other tricks where you never touch the opponent like rolling and slipping. The main purpose of using blocking defense is to reduce the impacts of the opponent's punch while absorbing the blow as much as you can. Sometimes, blocking is considered an inbuilt and default defense mechanism, as it doesn't require much energy and can be done easily. However, if the opponent throws a very strong punch, then you can be more harmful even if you block them with the right technique. The blocking technique is versatile as there are many ways to block your head, face, stomach, and square feet.

Clinching

Clinching is a defensive technique that is aimed at limiting the opponent or hugging within a closed quarter to restrict their ability to punch on the inside. Using the defensive trick of clinching with expertise, at the right time, and apt movement can lead to causing frustration in the mind of an opponent as each offense could easily go null and void. However, using enough clinching can cause the deduction of extra points or even disqualification of a fighter in some cases. This move can be an amazing defensive skill against an intimidating opponent, as you tie up their arms for a while until the referee interferes and gives instructions to separate both fighters.

Countering

As the name implies, countering is a trick to offense or counter offense a punch at your opponent. This defense technique emphasizes landing your punch to evade the opponent's punch. You can try simple hacks for countering like punching up straight cutting into the middle, which interrupts the opponent's attack, or a punch that could shift your head away from the attacking punch. The main idea behind this punching technique is to punch back to hurt your opponent, which could let you taste victory. When you go from a mode of defensive to offensive, it aggravates a strong whirl of aggression and power that helps you to throw a strong punch at the right time.

Chapter Six:

Perks of Practicing Boxing Workouts

Boxing is the ultimate challenge. There's nothing that can compare to testing yourself the way you do every time you step in the ring. —Sugar Ray Leonard

Nowadays, boxing workouts are becoming a widespread way of maintaining fitness and building stamina not only for boxers but for others, too. One can enjoy the benefits of this unique workout style, which includes improving one's dexterity, physical strength, and cardio. When practiced under proper guidance, this boxing fitness regime can be a fun-filled and rewarding challenge, which is making its place as one of the popular exercise forms. Different boxing workouts may vary a little bit from one another, depending on the trainers and the goal of the boxers, but the basics always remain the same. Moreover, researchers have revealed that boxing serves as a wonderful calorie-burning sport, which also helps in strengthening muscles and improving overall body metabolism. Thus, there are many favorable reasons for one to opt for boxing as a sport, a hobby, or simply as a workout technique. So, let's explore the different benefits of including boxing in one's life.

Improves Cardiovascular Health

Studies reveal that boxing has proven its advantages in boosting cardiovascular health by improving blood circulation and heart rate with its high-intensity moves. Regularly practicing boxing can help reduce the risk of various heart diseases, diabetes, and blood pressure fluctuations by strengthening heart muscles and relieving arterial tension. Moreover, it is also important for boxers to maintain a healthy heart condition, as it is one of the major factors used to rank them on the fitness scale, depending on their aerobic capacity. Thus, those who are ranked higher on the scale are considered healthier. One of the best cardio workouts for boxers is the jump rope, which supports building unimaginable endurance and strength in boxers. Apart from this, boxing demands a lot of moving around in the ring, hitting punches, and defending oneself. All these strenuous actions make the heart beat faster in order to supply oxygen and maintain the proper working of the body. On the whole, one can feel the blessings of a healthier heart in all the other aspects of life, which will eventually increase one's life expectancy.

Builds Muscles and Physical Strength

Boxing, which is known for its act of throwing punches and defending oneself, is not just a game of arms and upper body, instead, it needs the active participation of the entire body. In boxing, it is a must to stabilize your feet and lower body to efficiently take punches, in addition to the upper body strength required to endure the blow from the opponent. It is often misunderstood that the power of the punch is generated by the action of a tight fist and flexing shoulders alone, but the fact is that it is the outcome of flawless coordination of different core muscles and perfect moves. Thus, while in the training process, the coach will prepare the boxer with all sorts of strength-developing exercises like push-ups, pull-ups, squats, burpees, etc. All these vibrant moves and activities will provide good strength training to the boxers, thereby building their muscle power, boosting their overall stability, and endowing them with a well-toned strong body to become good boxers.

Develops Endurance

Endurance is one such trait of an individual that is a game changer when it comes to boxing, as it is a vital factor that can either make or break a fight. Boxing is a fighting art that requires tremendous effort from boxers to train themselves in terms of improving their stamina and building endurance. Thus, to learn the best boxing skills one must invest lots of precious time skipping ropes, running for miles, practicing high-intensity interval training, shadowboxing, etc. All of these exercises are beneficial for boosting steadiness and stamina in a boxer, which helps them make it to the end of the fight. However, building this unique feature is not an overnight miracle; instead, it is the collective effort of training, exercising regularly, and practicing patience, which surely yields excellence in the sport of boxing.

Enhances Mental Toughness

Boxing is thought to be a fierce physical sport, which demands great bodily strength and endurance. However, we often overlook the mental strength that it requires to stay strong and determined while taking punches from the opponent boxer. In other words, boxing is a game of discipline and self-control, which trains us to handle stressful situations strategically and smartly. Various sports psychologists have explained mental toughness as one's ability to cope with surrounding pressure and exhibit consistent performance as a boxer. A boxer, after undergoing hardcore and strenuous training, develops the basic skills and features that are required to become successful in this sport, but with the help of their trainers and psychologists, they can turn into a gem by exhibiting their mental strength in their game. Being human, it is very normal for every boxer to feel stress and anxiety just before a boxing match. But, with their mental toughness, they show tremendous courage while handling their emotions and situation with a great competitive spirit. Thus, the positive outlook of boxers motivates them to perform fabulously in the ring, against their toughest opponent.

Helps Maintain Overall Fitness

It is often challenging for many people to adhere to their fitness goals, as simply going for regular walks and hitting the gym may not give the desired results. Moreover, some people tend to neglect their fitness regime because of the failure to balance their professional and personal life. Many a time, following a regular schedule may end up leaving an individual bored and drained, thereby crushing their interest and enthusiasm to strive for a healthy and fit body. As boxing is a multitasking game that demands the involvement of the entire body, it can easily drive one toward overall fitness. Thus, by engaging in the active and adventurous sport of boxing, one can wisely invest their time, money, and efforts in achieving their long-term health goals and staying fit and strong.

Chapter Seven:

Tips to Learn Boxing for Newbies

Everybody thinks this is a tough man's sport. This is not a tough man's sport. This is a thinking man's sport. A tough man is gonna get hurt real bad in this sport. — Mike Tyson

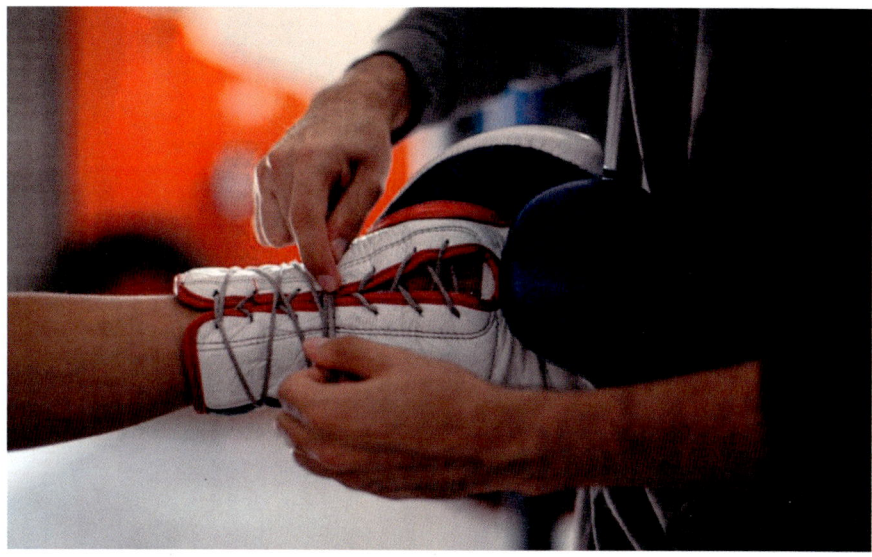

The journey toward learning boxing and becoming a renowned fighter is not always easy for all. There are many hurdles and challenges that one may face on the pathway to achieving their dreams. Many sorts of negativities like fear, confusion, lack of confidence, self-doubt, etc., may also surround an individual in this course of becoming a capable boxer. At such times, one needs to collect all their positive spirit and fight against all the odds by getting inspiration from their surrounding people and events. Thus, developing oneself by indulging in good habits and optimistic thoughts becomes the need of the hour. So, let's close our eyes and think wisely to find out the simple tips that can act as a trigger, which can push all the pessimism behind us, leading us toward excelling as a boxer.

Fight Your Fear

Like in every other sport, boxing has some sort of unseen fears associated with it. Every boxer would have definitely encountered these fears in the long and unique journey of boxing. Although not every fighter may accept the fact that their fear distracts and controls their minds negatively. At times, the intensity of this fear is such that even the most ferocious and powerful boxers tend to run away from their opponents. In the worst scenarios, it may even lead to the failure of the boxer in the ring. Fear is an unavoidable factor that can easily ruin one's performance, and thus, can act as an ultimate game-changer in a match. Fear is such a nasty emotion that cannot be washed off from our minds or suppressed by any means. The only way to overcome it is to stand strong, face your fears, and fight against all the odds that trigger the fear factor within you.

Fear is like a termite that ingrains into your mind and begins to eat away the hope, strength, skills, peace of mind, enthusiasm, and courage to win a game. In the context of boxing, fear has many faces, like fear of self-doubt, fear of getting critically injured, fear of being humiliated, fear of failure, and many more. Each person has different types of fear based upon their mindset and level of expertise in sports. Likewise, a beginner's mind has various fears that compel them to give up the urge to learn boxing. However, fighting against your fear is a mental game. Each one of us knows our fear and better understands the way to win over them. Therefore, instead of running away and giving up on your dreams to become a boxer, you must equip yourself to handle your fears intelligently. This eventually gets converted into power, vigor, and confidence to look beyond what is stopping us to achieve heights in our life.

Find Your Motivation

Boxing is an amazing sport that can help to make you feel rejuvenated, empower you with mental and physical endurance, and also support you in achieving health and fitness goals. More often, the idea to begin with boxing training sounds astounding which may even fill your mind with enormous energy, hopefulness, eagerness, enthusiasm, and positivity. However, sometimes during this endeavor putting in consistent efforts, struggling within yourself to accomplish the best results, and following the same routine could make you feel exhausted, lethargic, and worn out. These emerging negativities can make you feel weak and compel you to quit boxing training. Although, feeling lost, tired, and discouraged is quite common with every being. Instead of getting disheartened, one should look for a ray of hope that can help them to strive through and reach their set goals.

Thus, in times of low morale, looking at the life of famous professional boxers can act as a motivating example and help in filling up the required inspiration by reigniting the fire within us to continue learning boxing as our passion. The astonishing achievement of these great people who left no stone unturned to fill their future with fruits of success, name, and fame in the field of boxing is a true inspiration for all those who feel drained out in their endeavors. Therefore, the key to keeping going in times of distress and pessimistic thoughts is to search for better ways to motivate yourself that can help you rise and shine brighter. Different things work for different people. For some, it may be the glorious victory of their role model, while for others it may be the struggles of the inspirational fighters that helped them develop strength, endurance, and incomparable boxing skills.

Follow a Good Coach or Mentor

It will not be wrong to say that behind every successful boxer there is a hardworking mentor. Thus, searching for the best coach for yourself is the first thing one should go for in order to brush up on your boxing skills and evolve as a successful boxer. In haste to get oneself an expert coach, one needs to understand that there is nothing like an ideal coach. Different boxers require different types of training depending on their body type, specializations, and their desired way of boxing. In fact, many great boxers have more than one trainer, who guides and trains them toward mastering specific moves in boxing. A great boxing coach is the only person who has the capability to unlock your real potential, which can assist you in progressing and enjoying the pleasures of boxing. They are the ones who know you inside out, along with your abilities, your dreams, and the way you can achieve them. Thus, a trainer will act as a mirror who will reflect your true self, so that you can work on your weaknesses and build up your strengths to excel as a boxer.

As boxing is a physically and psychologically demanding sport, it requires a determined, optimistic, and well-organized coach, who can easily help you focus on your long-term boxing goals. Apart from all this, there are many other qualities that make up a good mentor like trust, bonding, supportive attitude, motivation, and effective communication. Thus, it's your trainer who is responsible for preparing you for the big fight in the ring safely, thereby helping you to bring your dreams to reality. Whatever your ultimate goals be, there is always a great experienced trainer there with you who works as a team. In the end, finding a boxing trainer for yourself will entirely be your own choice, depending on your chemistry and preferences, which can work magically to build your inner strength and boxing career as well. Apparently, it is a fact that the boxer jeopardizes his life in the arena, but it is the coach who invests his entire life and dynamism to fulfill the boxer's dreams and desires.

Eat a Healthy Diet

Just like every other sport, boxing when practiced as a passion needs a proper diet to maintain the fitness level of a boxer. Depending on the strategy and health of the boxer, the calorie intake must be managed to define a specific diet plan. Since boxing is a heavy-duty sport, the diet of a boxer must be consciously planned such that it provides them with energy for a longer time, helps them develop body mass, and assists them in gaining the required weight, along with the goodness of healing benefits. Thus, a balanced diet that is low in calories and rich in different vitamins, minerals, proteins, and carbohydrates is highly recommended for boxers. However, they can also take some amount of good saturated fats in the form of dry fruits, seeds, and nuts, as they are good for maintaining proper heart functioning.

A boxer must not only mind what they are eating but how they eat is also an important thing to be learned, as both starving and overloading oneself with too much food can restrict one from boxing efficiently. It is observed that following a three-meal plan for a day is not a feasible option for boxers, as it does not yield sufficient energy for undergoing training and practicing for the whole day. Thus, one can replace the standard three-meals-a-day plan with five or six meals in a day, which include two big meals paired with four smaller snack meals. This can therefore fulfill the energy demands for the entire day, thereby preventing the boxer from feeling hungry, even after the training sessions. Apart from eating a good diet, it is also necessary for the boxers to keep themselves hydrated by drinking sufficient fluids either in the form of water or energy drinks. So, if you opt to become a boxer, then counting on your calories, weighing yourself, and eating the right food are a few great tips to follow in order to excel in your sport.

Chapter Eight:

Tales of Famous Boxers

There are three things you need to remember in boxing, work hard, work harder, and work hardest. —Manny Pacquiao

Among all the known sports, boxing is one such thriving game that has the power to unleash the souls away from the negatives of life, thereby instilling attributes that can help in overcoming the odds and determining one's existence as a boxing legend. Boxing also has the capability to inspire people with its toughness and endurance, which can guide the boxers toward success and contentment in the sport and their lives, as well. Over the decades, there have been numerous significant names in the field of boxing and each boxer has their own presence in the ring, which marks their specific style and technique of boxing. However, the debate of who is the most amazing boxer of all time is something that has been an unsorted topic for ages. Boxing has served not only as a sport or a lifestyle change for these great boxers but, instead, it encompasses their entire life. For some, it is just a means of earning their living, while for others it is a matter of legacy and glory. So, let's dive deep into the lives of the most famous boxing legends to explore and understand the challenges they faced in the journey of their boxing career that made them their best versions.

Muhammad Ali

In the world of boxing, Muhammad Ali, an American heavyweight boxer, has earned his name and fame with great efforts and hard work. He not only excelled as a boxer but also stood strong against racism and equality of rights for all, which made him the talk of the town. Muhammad Ali proved himself by winning 56 fights out of 61, with 37 knockouts. Muhammad Ali had a unique boxing style, as he moved very differently in the ring, exhibiting tap-dance movement. His move is beautifully described in a quote, "Float like a butterfly, sting like a bee". On the whole, his artistic boxing style was a combination of his speed, his reflexes, and his heavy-weight body, thus making him a remarkable boxer. With his new techniques and elegance in the ring, he became a gold medalist in the Olympics and won the world championship three times.

He showed great endurance and toughness by taking punches in boxing matches with courage, thereby exhibiting his commitment and passion for boxing, which later on became his main attribute. After he retired from boxing, he was diagnosed with Parkinson's disease in 1983, which is probably considered to be due to the severe head injuries he received in the boxing arena. This hampered his speech and movement abilities, confining his boxing career. Despite all this, Muhammad Ali continued to be in the limelight as a public figure, working for humanitarian and charitable reasons. He expired at the age of 74, on 3rd June 2016, thus, marking his boxing legacy for his fans and lovers.

Mike Tyson

In the cradle of hardships of life, Mike Tyson was raised by a single mother and was left all alone after her death, when he was in his mid-teens. The suffering and pain that he endured at such a young age made him stronger than steel. Surrounded by difficulties and challenges, Mike Tyson was compelled to learn self-defense skills in his early years. As he had a difficult childhood and was often found involved in petty crime, he ended up in a juvenile home. But destiny had something else stored for him and thus, Bobby Stewart, an ex-boxer and a counselor at the juvenile justice home, realized Tyson's potential and introduced him to Cus D'Amato. He trained and launched Tyson into boxing and later became his legal guardian. In his early years of boxing, Tyson went on to win gold medals in the Junior Olympics in 1981 and 1982 and was given nicknames like "Iron Mike" and "Kid Dynamite."

Tyson had a very aggressive fighting style in the ring and was based on packing heavy punches. The secret behind this was his "peek-a-boo" style, which enabled him to move back and forth, thus reducing the space between his punch and the opponent boxer. This exceptional technique helped him to give crushing defeats to his big boxing competitors. Tyson's power is reinforced by the fact that he won 19 of his career's initial fights by knockout. Moreover, he earned himself a formidable reputation in the ring by defeating his opponents in the first round itself in many of the matches. His dominance in the ring made him the youngest boxer to acclaim the heavyweight title at just 20 years of age. Despite early success in the world of heavyweight championships, he found himself surrounded by various controversies in the latter part of his career, although he made a great comeback three years later. Tyson shares his legacy as an all-time great boxer, with 50 wins out of 58 matches in his unbeatable boxing career.

Rocky Marciano

If there is an undefeated champion in the world of heavyweight boxing, it is Rocky Marciano. Rocky had the sturdiest chin in boxing, famous for tolerating punch after punch from his opponents. Rocky himself had an immense endurance that was good enough to tire out his opponent; despite this, he has one of the highest knockouts to win ratio in his career. Rocky's parents were an immigrant from Italy who migrated to Massachusetts. Surprisingly, although good at sports, he was not inclined toward boxing. He spent his late teens working as a factory worker and later went on to enlist in the U.S. Army. His first encounter with boxing was when he got a chance to represent the U.S. Army at 23 years of age.

His road to greatness commenced when he started competing in amateur boxing competitions in Massachusetts. At the age of 29, Rocky contested his first championship match against Joe Walcott, which he went on to win by knockout. There was no looking back on him after that, as he went on to defend his title, out of which 6 were against Joe Walcott. At the peak of his career, Rocky decided to take retirement only at the age of 32 years due to his disturbed health conditions. Sadly, such a great boxer passed away in a plane crash just a day before his 46th birthday, marking the end of his life but making his existence everlasting in the world of boxing.

Sonny Liston

Sonny Liston was a formidable name in the domain of boxing, easily considered one of the greatest of all time. In fact, the Ring magazine has listed him as 10th in its greatest of all-time ranking. Sonny had a difficult childhood and suffered physical abuse at the hands of his father. The scars of this abuse were visible even after he grew up, with his body bearing marks of the whippings he received during his childhood. He started his amateur boxing career by winning the Intercity Golden Gloves championship. However, he had a hard time finding good sponsors for his professional boxing career, so he was forced to accept aid from people involved in shady business.

Liston was blessed with a well-built physique. He was tall and had a long reach, allowing him to smack his opponents, while being away from them. Liston went on to win the world heavyweight championship, but his career was surrounded by controversy related to his involvement in crime due to his sponsors. Unfortunately, Sonny had a heartbreaking end when he died in mysterious circumstances. His body was discovered several days later in a decomposed state in his Las Vegas home. However, Liston had a struggle-filled life, but he is remembered as a boxer with the biggest fist.

Boxing Memories

Conclusion

Boxing Training is an inspirational guide for all the boxing enthusiasts out there, who wish to learn and practice boxing as their hobby, passion, or sport. This book is ideal for training beginners, with all the basic fundamentals that are necessary to excel as a successful boxer. The book underlines all the potential factors that compel one to adopt boxing as an intact part of their life. It highlights the reasons that make boxing a highly preferred sport. It also covers the simple workouts and exercises that are important for a beginner to prepare them as great fighters in the boxing ring. As boxing is a hard-core physical sport, one needs to have complete knowledge of the different boxing gears that provide protection, support, and overall stability in the game. In this regard, the book delivers thorough information about the ways to use these gears and the benefits they provide to a boxer in the ring.

Moreover, this book will introduce the readers to unique and interesting boxing moves, including both punching and defending ones like the jab, hook, rolling, covering up, etc. The game of boxing is incomplete without the set of rules and regulations that are designed to assure a just and hustle-free match, which is vividly described in the book to provide clarity to the readers. Apart from this, the book will make the readers aware of the long-term benefits that boxing can have on one's personality, mental toughness, and physical strength. The book beautifully highlights the life stories of famous boxing legends and the way they stood strong and steady, taking punches and delivering the hardest ones to their opponents. All in all, this book is a life-changing treasure for all those who desire and dare to dream of evolving into one of the greatest boxers in the timeline.

At last, I would wholeheartedly thank all the readers who showed great interest to explore and understand the different specifications related to boxing and spared their precious time to read the book. I appreciate the willpower within you that has driven you to fight your fears and dilemmas by adopting a path that will lead toward achieving your dreams as a boxer. Furthermore, I am very excited to read your reviews about the book, as your feedback is very precious and can guide and motivate me to write down more such engrossing books. So, let's dive deep into the depth of our minds, to unlock the hidden interesting questions that can bring us closer to boxing:

- Is boxing an ideal sport for me?
- Can I become a great boxer?
- Do I have the stamina and strength to pursue boxing?
- How will boxing change my life?
- Who is my favorite all-time boxer?
- Is boxing a difficult sport to learn?
- What is the first step I should take to become a boxer?
- What gears I must have to learn boxing safely?

Now, the wait is over, and you have a chance to make your dream come true by grabbing this book and learning all the necessary things required to embrace the thrill and enthusiasm associated with boxing in your life.

References

Admin. (2018, September 5). *The essential equipment for boxing beginners.* Made 4 Fighters. https://made4fighters.com/blogs/equipment-guides/boxing-equipment-for-beginners

Bedosky, L. (2023, January 5). *Boxing workouts: Definition, health benefits, and getting started.* Everyday Health. https://www.everydayhealth.com/fitness/boxing-workouts/guide/

British Boxers. (2016, August 23). *Inspirational boxing quotes.* British Boxers. https://www.britishboxers.co.uk/2016/08/inspirational-boxing-quotes/

Dilbert, R. (2017, October 27). *Theodore Roosevelt: The rough-and-tumble, wrestling, grappling president.* Bleacher Report. https://bleacherreport.com/articles/2559772-theodore-roosevelt-the-rough-and-tumble-wrestling-grappling-president

Duquette, T. (2021, July 16). *6 basic punches every boxer needs to know.* Join Fight Camp. https://blog.joinfightcamp.com/training/six-6-basic-boxing-punches/

Edwards, T. (2021, August 27). *6 benefits of boxing for fitness.* Healthline. https://www.healthline.com/health/fitness/boxing-benefits

Head, J. (2010, November 21). *Mike Tyson: His childhood and early boxing years.* Bleacher Report. https://bleacherreport.com/articles/523260-boxing-mike-tyson-and-the-early-years

Editors. (2009, December 16). *Muhammad Ali*. History. https://www.history.com/topics/black-history/muhammad-ali

ISSA. (2022, September 20). *Top benefits of a boxing workout and why you should try it*. Issa Online. https://www.issaonline.com/blog/post/top-benefits-of-a-boxing-workout-and-why-you-should-try-it

Jamie. (2020, February 2). *50 inspiring boxing quotes to get you motivated*. My Boxing Life. https://myboxinglife.com/50-inspiring-boxing-quotes-to-get-you-motivated/

Jarvis, K. (2023, January 1). *Boxing rules: The definitive guide of boxing regulation 2023*. The Karate Blog. https://thekarateblog.com/boxing-rules/

Keller, D. (2021, November 18). *The day in the life of a boxer*. Boxing Highs. https://boxinghighs.com/blogs/news/the-day-in-the-life-of-a-boxer

Krishna. (2019, March 6). *A guide to perfecting the boxers diet*. Super Prof. https://www.superprof.co.in/blog/what-is-a-boxers-diet/#:~:text=Boxers%20need%20more%20nutrients%20to

Leahy, S. (2013, January 27). *Danny Jacobs and the 5 most inspirational boxing stories*. Bleacher Report. https://bleacherreport.com/articles/1500441-danny-jacobs-and-the-5-most-inspirational-boxing-stories

Mccarthy, P. (2021, December 10). *At-home boxing equipment & gear for beginners*. Join Fight Camp. https://blog.joinfightcamp.com/boxing-equipment/what-equipment-do-you-need-to-start-boxing/

N, J. (2008, June 20). *16 basic boxing tips. How to box*. ExpertBoxing. https://expertboxing.com/16-basic-boxing-tips

Piccioto, E. D. (2018, November 29). *Muhammad Ali – He was great, but was he the greatest?* The Perspective. https://www.theperspective.com/debates/sports/muhammad-ali-great-greatest#:~:text=The%20combination%20of%20his%20heavyweight

Staff, P. (2018, July 14). *What is Boxing?* Puncher Media. https://punchermedia.com/what-is-boxing-the-hard-hitting-combat-sport-explained/

Stewart, J. (2016, September 4). *9 essential boxing equipment for beginners: What to get and why.* Warrior Punch. https://warriorpunch.com/boxing-equipment/

Stone, C. (2020, December 24). *Quick history of boxing: Origins and interesting facts.* Legends Boxing. https://www.legendsboxing.com/post/boxing-history

Vladisavljevic, V. (2020, May 27). *The 4 basic types of boxing punches: Everything you need to know.* way of martial arts. https://wayofmartialarts.com/the-4-basic-types-of-boxing-punches/

Walker, D. (2019, February 14). *What makes a good boxing trainer: A complete guide.* WBCME. https://www.wbcme.co.uk/ringside/what-makes-a-good-boxing-trainer/

Image References

Alexandru, C. (2022, February 27). *Women fighting on a boxing match* [Online Image]. Pexels. https://www.pexels.com/photo/women-fighting-on-a-boxing-match-11313292/

Danilyuk, P. (2020a, December 26). *A man in black shirt wearing yellow hand wraps* [Online Image]. Pexels. https://www.pexels.com/photo/a-man-in-black-shirt-wearing-yellow-hand-wraps-6295797/

Danilyuk, P. (2020b, December 26). *Men on the floor stretching* [Online Image]. Pexels. https://www.pexels.com/photo/men-on-the-floor-stretching-6295713/

Hopper X, I. (2022, December 21). *Boxer in head guard and gloves* [Online Image]. Pexels. https://www.pexels.com/photo/boxer-in-head-guard-and-gloves-14840775/

Keller, J. (2018, March 24). *Two fighters doing sparring match* [Online Image]. Pexels. https://www.pexels.com/photo/two-fighters-doing-sparring-match-960799/

Muertos Crew, L. (2021, July 19). *A person tying the laces of a boxing glove* [Online Image]. Pexels. https://www.pexels.com/photo/a-person-tying-the-laces-of-a-boxing-glove-8810063/

Nilov, M. (2021, February 7). *Painting of a boxer on wall* [Online Image]. Pexels. https://www.pexels.com/photo/painting-of-a-boxer-on-wall-6739947/

Piacquadio, A. (2020, March 1). *Muscular sportsman doing plank exercise on kettlebells More info Share* [Online Image]. Pexels. https://www.pexels.com/photo/muscular-sportsman-doing-plank-exercise-on-kettlebells-3837433/

Made in the USA
Coppell, TX
27 May 2025